Best Friends Forever

Written and compiled by
Carly Warner

Illustrated and designed by
Amy Dietrich

Peter Pauper Press, Inc.
White Plains, New York

May your room always be
too small to hold all of your
friends.

$\mathcal{I}$ can trust my friends. . . .
These people force me to
examine myself, encourage
me to grow.

Cher

$\mathcal{L}$ots of people want to ride with you in the limo, but what you want is someone who will take the bus with you when the limo breaks down.

Oprah Winfrey

$\mathcal{A}$ true friend is on call 24/7.

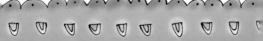

A BFF is your own personal
guardian angel!

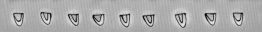

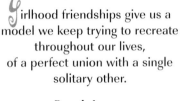

*G*irlhood friendships give us a
model we keep trying to recreate
throughout our lives,
of a perfect union with a single
solitary other.

Beverly Lowrey

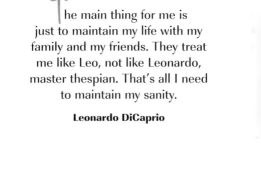

The main thing for me is just to maintain my life with my family and my friends. They treat me like Leo, not like Leonardo, master thespian. That's all I need to maintain my sanity.

Leonardo DiCaprio

We love each other like sisters. If Marisa's experiencing happiness, I can almost just ride on her coattails and experience it with her.

Ashley Jones

It's rare to find someone you get on with so well. He was my best friend on the show for five years. George (Clooney) could finish my sentences for me.

Julianna Margulies

*M*ates (friends) are important.
Very Australian. True-blue.

Patrick Rafter

$\mathcal{B}$oy friends come and go, but
girl friends are forever.

Friends get you through bad times and help you enjoy the good times.

 I don't need much. I need my
friends, my dogs, my family,
my music.

Ricky Martin

You know what's good? To have somebody ground you and say, "Wait, it's okay."

Jennifer Aniston

$\mathcal{E}$very girl had her niche. One girl was a great cross-country runner, one was a talented painter. It made me feel like I was just one of the girls, not strange or isolated. I was very lucky to have such nice friends.

Reese Witherspoon,
on her high school years

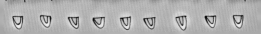

Friendship is knowing the right thing to say, and knowing when to say nothing at all.

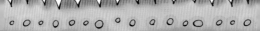

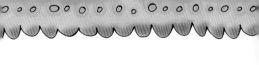

I keep my friends out of the public eye. Acting makes me happy, but it's not my whole life.

Sarah Michelle Gellar

Right now [I love] just talking on the phone with my friends. I like to find out what's going on with everyone so that when I go back, I'm not completely out of it.

Tatyana Ali

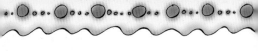

One of my favorite things
in the world is girls' night out.

Lisa Ling

[A best friend] never tells you
"Do this" or "Do that" but is there
for you and will be straight up if
you are totally wrong.

Amy Jo Johnson

*S*he's such an inspiration to me.

Gwendolyn Sanford,
about her friend Amy Jo Johnson

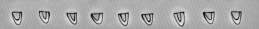

If men want to introduce her
(Meg Ryan) to their mothers,
women want to be her
best friend.

Judith Newman

$\mathcal{A}$ best bud is the only cure
for a bad breakup.

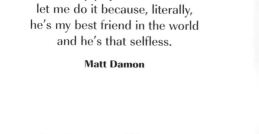

𝓘 look at my role
(in *Good Will Hunting*) and I
think that Ben (Affleck) could
have easily played it. I think he
let me do it because, literally,
he's my best friend in the world
and he's that selfless.

Matt Damon

[What does make you feel good about yourself] is the continuity of your friendships and how you're communicating in your relationship . . .

Rachel Griffiths

I'm not a celebrity to [my friends]. They don't care. They slap me in the back of the head when I mess up. They try to help me out when I need it, which is a lot. They take care of me.

Luke Perry

She (Heather Locklear) was the glue that held the set together. Everyone loved her; they would do anything for her.

James Darren

$\mathcal{D}$on't judge your bud unless
you have been in her position.

Friends are important because they are the ones who are there for you when you are in need of security and advice. They accept you for you and make your life more fun and exciting.

Susan Dunn, age 18

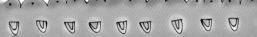

*L*isten, really listen,
to your best friend's whining—
even if she's going on and on
about her jerky ex-boyfriend a
year after they've broken up.

Lisa Nicole Carson

We had to [bond off-screen] because I saw the relationship that we had on camera and it seemed so real. It really seemed like we were friends, best friends. Before the movie, we hung out together, and in between takes, I would comb her hair and she would play with my braids. We were friends.

Brandy,
on Jennifer Love Hewitt

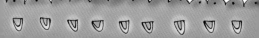

A friend recognizes your mistakes but is kind enough to forget them.

The funnest thing
is having my friends and sisters
over and cooking, hanging out,
and talking.

Natasha Gregson Wagner

ℓ got by because I was a pretty good student and had one or two friends here and there who were either older or down-to-earth.

Natasha Lyonne

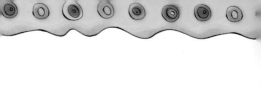

A BFF is the ONLY person
who can tell you that you look fat
in those pants!

I'm constantly looking for friends, for girlfriends. Whenever I see a girl that might be a friend, I just lose it. I'm like, "She is sooo nice. Look how sweet she is."

Alicia Silverstone

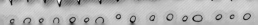

𝒥 don't think I could have survived these eight years without my friends. They took such good care of me when I felt alone.

Jennifer Grey

It wasn't until an uncle of mine emigrated to Canada, leaving behind an old Spanish guitar with five rusty strings, that my enormous and clumsy fingers found a musical home, and I found what was to be my best friend.

Sting

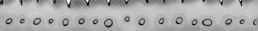

The best thing a BFF ever did for me was to make me a memory book of all the things that we have shared together.

Zoë Auerbach, age 13

The best gift that a BFF can give
is her time, her self.

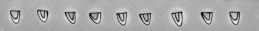

I adore her (Alicia Witt). Alicia and I have these unbelievable emotional/psychological/professional/intellectual/spiritual conversations.

Dedee Pfeiffer

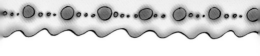

𝒪f me and my girls go out for dinner, that's a big deal. We're all calling each other all day like, "What are you gonna wear? Where should we go? Who's driving?"

Jennifer Lopez

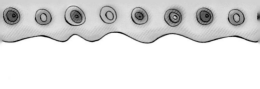

 just want to hang with my
friends.

Britney Spears

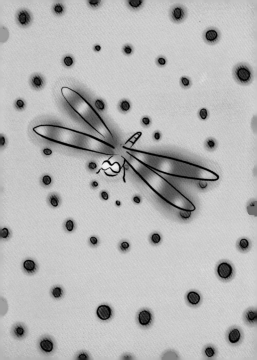

*G*ossip is that much more interesting coming from your best bud!

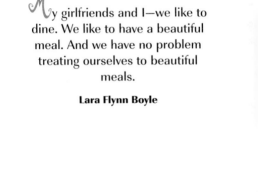

*M*y girlfriends and I—we like to dine. We like to have a beautiful meal. And we have no problem treating ourselves to beautiful meals.

Lara Flynn Boyle

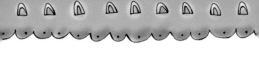

The bottom line with me is fun. I enjoy life, I enjoy people. And people—black, white, Asian, or alien—enjoy that energy.

Will Smith

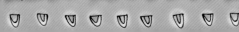

What I look for in a friend is someone who is there to listen whenever you need her and is continually supportive.

Melanie Temkin, age 17

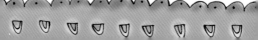

$\mathcal{M}$atthew (Matt Lillard) is my friend. And when you work with somebody who you already have a relationship with and who you trust, you can't help but do great work with that person.

Freddie Prinze, Jr.

$\mathcal{F}$riendship is telling someone
what they don't have the courage
to tell themselves.

My BFF is always there to tell
me I can do anything I want to if I
just believe in myself and set my
mind to whatever I want to do.

Nadine Johns, age 24

You can't expect one friend to
fulfill all your needs. You have to
find different people and pick
who you talk to about what.

Hope Boonshaft

$\mathcal{L}$ike snowflakes, each friend is
a precious gift. No two are
exactly alike.

I . . . love being in Big Bear with friends. . . . That's the one thing I look forward to every year, because it's with all my closest friends. It's great.

Sean Hayes

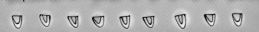

*D*rew has a more sincere instinct for giving than anyone of our generation I've met in this business. She has forged this terrific positivity toward life, and a spiritual density and grace, out of nothing.

Edward Norton,
on Drew Barrymore

I really value [Calista Flockhart's] friendship—she was like a sister to me—especially because it's harder to make friends with girls than with guys.

Melissa Joan Hart

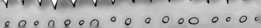

A friend listens to what you say. A BFF listens to what you don't have to say.

A friend laughs with you, but a best friend cries with you.

$\mathcal{M}$y friends and the people
around me have never changed
and I am immensely
grateful for that.

Kate Winslet

Most of my friends are completely out of the business. Just friends from high school and my neighborhood.

Eddie Kaye Thomas

We (the cast of our show) all get along so well, and think there is a really good quality of person. A very genuine, real thing going on.

Keri Russell

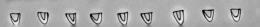

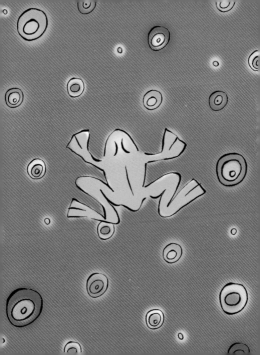

$\mathcal{M}$y college fantasy is sitting underneath a tree on campus with my glasses on and having a cool guy friend study with me, but he's just a friend—you know, that college thing where he becomes a friend for life.

Jennifer Love Hewitt

The best thing a friend ever did for me was give me a huge hug just at the right time.

Melanie Temkin, age 17

We all have our differences of opinion but we're the best of friends.

Chris Kirkpatrick,
'N Sync

[Sandra Bullock] has helped me so much. She is really fun and special, and has a great point of view. She never really gives advice, but she talks about her experience and what she has learned from it and what she would do differently. She has told me what to expect. She has really, really been a great friend.

Matthew McConaughey

A friend will defend you even
if you're wrong — because
anyone can defend you when
you're right!

In your heart you possess the key to friendship; nurture it well.

*A*s girls, we are willing to give even the biggest toad of a guy a chance in hopes he'll become a prince. Who knows how many new BFF's you might have if you give a couple of your fellow girlfrogs the same shot.

Karen Bokram,
Publisher, *Girls' Life* magazine

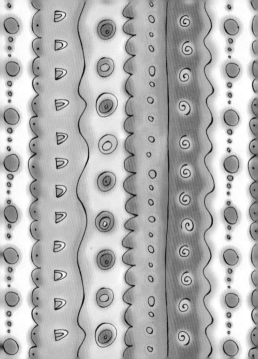